3

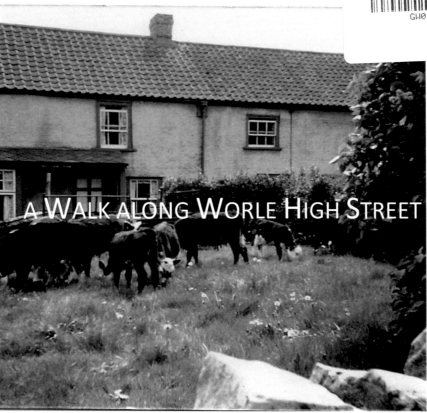

WORLE

HISTORY

SOCIETY

A WALK ALONG WORLE HIGH STREET

In pictures and words: Raye Green

Published by Honey Pot Press
2 The Dell, Worle, BS22 9LZ
1st published 2011
This edition 2012
ISBN 978-0-956 9752-3-2

This gentle stroll along our High Street is, I must admit, a self-indulgence. I grew up in this street from the time I was three until I married, and I always loved it. Some of the pictures are wonderfully clear, others are very old and look it, but I could not bring myself to leave them out.

Many of the photographs are from my parents' collection, some were taken with the family Box Brownie, and some were passed on to me by kind friends.

The words are all my own, so I must apologise at once for any errors, and beg you to let me know kindly. I really do do my best. Enjoy the walk.

Raye Green

The Square Wells

4

Let us start our walk along Worle High Street which, by the beginning of the 20th century, had overtaken the 'top road' in commercial importance. The old masterpiece on the opposite page was taken by someone with the foresight to realise that one day it would become a treasure. It was probably taken around the year 1909, and the camera would have been mounted on a tripod standing in the middle of the road. It is facing west and the photographer was no doubt hidden under the necessary black cloth, used to shut out the daylight.

It has attracted considerable attention from the men folk. The gent on the left is wearing a fetching hat, and sports a considerable white moustache. He is, I assume a workman, as he is leaning on a spade. He has removed his coat and is in his shirt sleeves, so maybe it is a warm day. The windows of the New Inn public house on the left are open, too, and there is a strong shadow from the chimney on the roof of the laundry from the sun which was in the south west. There is foliage on the trees.   The two likely lads on the right are posing happily. I suspect that the chap with the workmanlike broom also spotted the camera and looked as busy as possible for the shot. He would be standing in the middle of the ghastly mini roundabout if we moved him forward 100 years. The two horse drawn vehicles seem to be loaded with assorted wood. Telegraph poles have begun to appear in the village. The area in the picture was known as The Square.   The cross roads, even back in 1909, offered the choice of turning left down Station Road. The small sign on the curved wall says 'Light Railway' and there is a direction arrow. The 'ALACE ESTON' sign is advertising a twice nightly production at the Albany Palace [later renamed the Tivoli], confirmed by the sign on the shop wall on the other side of the road. One could turn right up the Scaurs past the shop window with the Fry's Chocolate advertisements, or carry straight on beyond the pub and the malthouse and along the High Street.

The cottages on the right and the laundry on the corner of Station Road are long gone, but the pub, now named the Woodspring, does look much better cared for a hundred years later.

6

We are still looking at The Square, but this is not such a clear picture and it is looking east, back in the other direction towards the New Inn pub on the far right. Interestingly, there is still a bicycle propped up against the pub wall.

The solitary gent is looking towards the camera, but it is impossible to tell what kind of day it was. There are no shadows. The 1901 census gives the publican of the New Inn as Mr George Smith, then aged 60 years, so it is just possible that he was still in charge, although 69 years old is quite an age for a licensee at that time. Other details in the same census give houses numbered 1 to 18 in The Square, which surprised me. Where exactly, did The Square start and end, I wonder.

We can see the shop window on the left, but I can't read the notice above it. Again, there is an open window, and the boundary wall is need of repair by the look of it. Has there been some sort of minor accident? Certainly, the gas lamp standard is at a rakish angle.

The village pump was positioned against the wall of the cottage in the centre of the picture, but it is not possible to see it.

If we were to follow the road straight on past the New Inn we would see the cottages on the left which were demolished in 1939, when the Rose Garden was established with some considerable fanfare.

Before we move on, let us look at a later view of The Square.

8

Fifty years has made a difference. This photograph was taken by John May in the early 1950s, using his aunt's Box Brownie camera. No tripod or black cloth for John, but still a very successful snapshot, taken with his back to the New Inn. He was a boy at the time and his only interest was in the No. 40 green 'bus. The buses ran every ten minutes up and down the High Street. This spot in The Square at the east end of our route was the 'bus terminus and this one had turned around in the small space and was facing west, with one passenger already on board, waiting to depart for its destination in Moorland Road. Haywards' Military Pickle is a treat I do not recall. The buses often waited in this spot for 10 minutes and the driver and conductor would alight and smoke a cigarette, or open a flask of tea and eat a sandwich. The cottage behind the 'bus, on the right of the photograph, is familiar to us now. It appears in the previous picture, but by the 1950s the rendering seems to have been given some attention.

Behind the limestone garden wall on the left is a traditional Somerset stone cottage with brick details above the windows and a little pointed porch over the front door. The garden has a small outbuilding – a kind of shed with a flat roof, which is actually a pigeon loft. Another one of John's photos from the same spot shows a washing line full of white sheets in the front garden.

If we set off along the High Street in the same direction that the 'bus is about to take, we can stop and have a peep at one the shops on the south side of the road.

10

I always loved this muddily bit of architecture. Old Somerset cottages were often built side-on to the road, like the one on the left, and often had a small courtyard. This yard is protected from the road by railings, supported by concrete posts. They were, I remember, very good for swinging on. On this south side of the road the front windows saw very little sun, so I am not surprised to see Mr. Griffin standing outside his cycle shop with a friend, catching a few cheering rays. This is an undated picture, but the camera is still rare enough to attract a quick pose.

The shop was really very small and I assume it was built on as an adjunct to the original cottage. Although, the old stone wall on the right looks original, so perhaps I am quite wrong. The roof of the shop is very attractive, and reminds me of the type supplied with 'Bayko Building Sets' – a favourite children's toy in the 1950s. The shop is conveniently placed for Miss Griffin to keep an eye on Wilf Kingsbury, who lived almost opposite in Banwell House, and whom she later married.

My first memory of this shop is during the period when it was a news agency, run by Percy Prewitt and his family, in the early 50s. Sadly, the whole row was demolished in the late 1960s and the block now occupied by Proper Job was built in its place.

The weather is holding up for us, so let's walk a little further west, past the Lamb Inn, where the street turns a little to the south, and see what we can find.

11

12

We have walked past the Lamb Inn now and are looking to our right, up Lawrence Road and back into the first decade of the 20th century again. The novelty of the camera is obvious. The five youngsters at the bottom of the road are fascinated and two more are on their way down to join in.

The overwhelming impression of this picture is the beauty of the limestone from our local quarry in Kewstoke Road. Cottages and garden walls, built of matching stone, were a major feature of the old village until after World War 2. The detail in the architecture of the cottages on the left is worth special notice. The bays are adorned with castellations. It must have been possible to climb out of the sash windows upstairs onto the little ledge – hardly a balcony- above the sitting room bay. The front gardens may have been small, but their gateways were flanked by stone pillars with carved limestone tops.

On the right hand side we can see the entrance into a builder's yard and further up again is the Methodist Church, often called Ebenezer, where the History Society meets in AD 2011. The cottages at the top of the hill and the foliage complete this lovely English scene, which is probably my favourite.

Well, turn around and carry on along the road, please.

14

We seem to have hit upon some excitement here. Worle's last ever carnival queen, Margaret Wilcox, is being driven along the High Street on Whitsun Monday afternoon in 1956. She is looking over towards the camera which is being held by her grandmother, Mrs. Neathway, who is standing in her own front garden at the bakery. Margaret's sister, Jean is the girl on the right, sitting on the garden wall. The carnival floats and walkers are heading along to the Square, where they will turn right into Station Road, down the side of the New Inn, and thence to the Recreation Ground, where tea and beer and stalls, a marquee and dancing will await them.

The three cottages in the background are 'Greenwood Cottages', so much more picturesque than the small supermarket that replaced them – currently the Co-operative, by the way. The Edwards family, local farmers, lived in one of the cottages and occasionally their calves could be seen grazing in the front gardens. The three families who lived in the cottages used their back rooms much more than the ones at the front. The back was sunny and cheerful. The front looked cute, with the small roof extending the length of the terrace above the little square bay windows, but the rooms were dark and rather dismal.

To the right of the cottages was a five bar gate and a lane, used by the dairy herd to make their way to and from the fields behind for milking.

Now we are going to turn our backs on the cottages and the carnival queen to look at the other side of the road.

16

...And we see that Mrs. Neathway's bakery is for sale. It must be the 1970s, and Barlow Hiles and Co. are certainly making the best of the prime position. This lovely house was such a loss. It was demolished, of course, and replaced by a ghastly modern block of shops with a dance studio above. The photograph is in colour, but the price of printing being what it is, we see it in black and white.

On the brow of the hill, to the left is the spire of St. Martin's Church and we can see the roofs of the old stone buildings mingling happily with the chalet style houses in Church Road.

The bakery was such a warm, friendly place and the smell permeated the area when the ovens were on. You approached the kitchens by walking up the driveway on the left of the house. The door was round the back, which was very convenient for my family, as my father rented the garage on the far left of this picture from Mrs. Neathway. Each morning he would walk up to get the car and in evening he would park it again, and pop in for the bread.

The front garden was a generous size and often used for celebrations. In particular, the VE day party is well remembered and was well photographed, but this is intended to record the High Street, so we must move on along towards the west and back again in time.

The Parade, Worle.

18

Doctor Who, eat your heart out. We are in 1909. Two very well dressed, tidy children are glancing politely at the photographer, who is in the middle of the road again, tripod and all, without fear of traffic! Actually, if we came forward 100 years again, he would be right opposite the 'bus stop and not far from the zebra crossing.

In the distance is the Lamb Inn where we stopped to look up Lawrence Road on page 12. Neathways Bakery is out of sight, back from the road on the left beyond the row of terraced cottages. 53 years later the carnival queen would have just travelled along here, but there would have been pavements, and hopefully no horse manure!

The cottages, of local stone, of course, were and are a joy. I love the regular repetition of the chimneys, the bedroom windows and the bays. The little houses face south and catch the sun all day long. Each cottage had a name: Avonia, The Roses, The Laurels and so on. They also had the great convenience of The Parade, directly opposite. This row of shops with living accommodation above provided everything from an ironmongery, post office, haberdashery and grocery to a fishmongers and greengrocers. The butchers' shop was at the far end of the terrace on the left. You can just see the white awning. How much better than a supermarket!

On the right you can see the sun flooding into the road from the gap where Mendip Avenue joins the High Street. For very many years Mendip Avenue was a small no-through road, leading to the infants' school and the Village Club, and very little else.

Crowd watching the Unveiling Ceremony of Clock Tower at Worle. 413.

20

Something happened to everyone's world in the ten years between the photograph on page 18, and this one. That thing was World War 1, and our village suffered as much as any. Sons, fathers and brothers were lost and the bereaved people needed some special way of remembering. They raised money for a memorial with a clock tower marking the hours since the Armistice. On this day in 1919 everyone was there to see the unveiling of the War Memorial, which is still such a treasure to us all. The people, on this day, assumed that the peace was for ever. The Great War had been the war to end all wars.

It looks as if it was a grey day and, in the fashion of the time, men and women alike wore hats to show their respect. There were ironwork gates on the memorial when it was new, but these were not locked, so people were able to go in and look at the names of the boys and men who would not grow old.

The walkway outside the shops in The Parade was full of mourners. In the background we can see a brand new sign stating 'Skidmore and Sons' protruding above the corner shop, and another advertising 'Royal Daylight Oil'. Mr. Dunning was already ensconced in the Post Office. The sash windows above Skids' shop are open, and I dare say Old Mr and Mrs Skid were watching proceedings – not that they were old then. The birth of the twins, Bill and Bert, was still seven years away.

It would be good to know the name of the elegant lady, dressed in light coloured clothes and sitting in the bath chair.

The Parade. Worle. 918.

22

We don't need to move to admire this picture, except in time. When this was put in the Mercury a gentleman, named Colin Bennett, wrote in to say that he was the baby in his mother's arms outside the Post Office, and therefore the picture was taken in 1933.

There is a family group making the most of the photo opportunity outside Skids. There seem to be a girl and two little boys, who would be about seven years old. I wonder if the boys are Bill and Bert. One of them is proudly sporting a scooter. Apart from Skidmores, the other shops have signs saying, I think, P. R. Boxer, Clarke, Co-operative Society Ltd. and Dunning. Each establishment had display windows either side of a central door. The pavement is quite well swept, but although the High Street is made up and looked after by the Council, the entrance to Mendip Avenue is unsurfaced and consists of rough stone.

The other side of the street has a pavement right along to the Lamb Inn, with a very effective looking curb stone. Although there are no cars in this photo, the roads would have been shared by horse drawn vehicles and motor vehicles at this time.

I wonder if youngsters will ever grow out of their interest in cameras. I'll try it on a busy day in the High Street and see what reaction I get.

23

24

We are looking towards Weston now, with the Mendip Avenue junction on the left. All the houses in the terrace on the left still have their stone walls and gate posts. The property on the corner had rather elegant arched windows in those days and was operating as a bank. I like the doorway, angled across the corner.

On the right hand side of the road, the taller stone walls are still intact. The gateway is impressive because it is the entrance to what was then the Vicarage, later it was renamed ' Kirklands' when the vicars of Worle moved to the house in Church Road, looking down Coronation Road.

This picture must have been taken before World War 1, possibly in 1909 again. The fashion of the day supports that date.

The sunny day has brought people out. In the distance, a woman is standing by a small stall, or maybe a stool, and it looks as if she is selling something. The cart is loaded with hay. Further in the distance there is a house, rather a grand one, on the hillside, and there is a cottage which I think has disappeared.

Pavements seem to be appearing on both sides of the street, though the one on the right is still work in progress.

What season of the year was this taken? The trees are contradictory. I think it is winter. If you enlarge the picture enough the leaves on the right are actually ivy, but what species is the tree on the left?

26

Now we know exactly where we are, and when. The date is the 20th August, 1939; the camera is situated in the bay window of the upstairs flat at 'Sandringham', High Street. The ground floor is occupied by Bessell and Raike's, the Chemist Shop. My grandparents, William and Rachel Jones later lived in the flat. The gardens in the bottom right corner belong the adjoined properties, called 'Windsor' and 'Cumberland' and the odd circular feature in the very corner is an advertising sign fixed to the wall of the chemist shop.

We are looking at a village steeling itself for War. This is the first Church Parade that the scouts, guides and brownies took part in. The eighty young people were led out of Mendip Avenue by the Boys' band and marched up Coronation Road and along Church Road to St. Martins' Church. The flags are flying and the drums are beating out the rhythm. Villagers are watching and walking with them. Everyone must have had their hearts in their mouths.

Despite the times, it is good to see the stone walls as they used to be. There is even a pillar still standing, which would have provided the entrance to the Old, old Vicarage. I see that they finished off the pavements nicely.

The orchard is still in full leaf where the Health Centre now stands. I recall the blossom on the apple trees, which was glorious in April.

If we look up to the hill behind the cottages and the war memorial, we can see the oldest part of Worle, looking down to see what's happening.

28

Here, I have to apologise for the quality of the photography. I was about 7 when I took this snap.

It is 1953 and we are standing on the pavement now, looking at Bessell and Raikes' chemist shop, with the Ilford sign, which hung there for 20 years or more. Notice the electric clock in the window, which my family and many others relied upon to provide accurate time, day in, day out.

The first house, in dire need of some paint, is 'Windsor', where I grew up. That bay window was our sitting room when this was taken. Six members of my family lived in the house at this time: my grandparents, Norman and May Charles; my parents, Mervyn and Betty Jones; my uncle, Wyn Charles, and me.   Next to Windsor is Mrs. Wilmot's home – 'Cumberland', and beyond that is the Co-operative butchers and then the grocery department. Shopping was a doddle living there, and I regret the changes.

The terrace was built in 1897, I believe, by Mr Phippen snr. All the houses had front gardens in those days, which you can see by taking a look back at the picture on page 24, which shows the terrace towards the left of this photograph.

The shadows are sharp and demonstrate all too clearly, that the houses face north, so all the warmth and brightness came in the back windows. It was, however, a wonderful place to grow up, watching *everything* that went on.

Some brave photographer is in the middle of the road again and there are a few more cars about than in earlier shots. The vehicles look as if they are about late 1940s models and the woman with the bicycle does not seem worried about standing the street. The gas lamp on the far right looks well cared for. We are looking east towards the Lamb Inn.

I have blown up parts of this photograph to have a closer look, and there seems to be a union flag flying outside Neathway's Bakery on the left of the street, and more flags above the shops in The Parade. People seem to be gathered on the Parade, chatting. So it could be that we are looking at the V.E. day decorations in 1945, or even the Coronation preparations in 1953. Can anyone tell us? I have seen versions of this picture which show the pram on the far left accompanied by a nurse maid in her uniform, so perhaps 1945 is a better bet.

One of the cottages on the north side of the street is for sale. Again, it is possible to see from an enlarged version, that it is the one on the corner of Hill Road.

Does that car in the foreground belong to Mr. Vowles, I wonder?

Take a good look at the low garden wall on the left and see if you can spot it in the next photograph, when we travel back in time again.

This is a delightful shot, taken by a very patient photographer, I suspect. Either that or a very lucky one. It gives us a chance to consider three possible ways of getting along the High Street.

The lady and her Pomeranian dog are using the oldest and best way, Shank's Pony, and they appear winning the race. The car, of course, is parked at the curb, which is still happily devoid of yellow lines.   The number plate, made up of two letters and four numbers, tell us that the make of car was discontinued in 1932. The jalopy in the picture must have been getting on in years – probably about 25 years old.

The bottle green 40 'bus is one of the newer models and may well have just pulled away from the 'bus stop outside the old Co-op store.

Although the road was still relatively quiet and has no zebra crossings at this time, it is no longer possible for the photographer to stand in the middle of the road to take the picture.

So, it is the first decade of the 20th century. The Golden Lion Hotel is easily recognisable on the left with its odd little trellised porch.   There is a lion, painted gold and couchant above the porch. The lion has now disappeared, but I have no idea when or where he went.

No doubt, you have spotted the low garden wall, but there are some great differences elsewhere. There is a cottage still standing next to the Golden Lion and a rather American looking hoarding with an advertisement pasted on to it. The big tree in the centre of this picture has disappeared in the later one on page 30 – either that or it has been cut back and has re-grown as a different species.

The dear old Ford car on the right is a very early model and would have been quite a novelty and only for the very well off.   The cart in the foreground was a much more usual sight, and even that is a rather superior, four wheeled model.

The little boys looking straight into the camera are very clear, almost recognisable, but I have no names for them, or for the girl. I am also hopelessly ill informed about when the telegraph poles were erected.

It seems that this stretch of the street was a popular spot for photographers through the years. This one was facing west, with the Golden Lion on the right and a two-wheeling cart this time, with its driver standing for the shot! My eye has been drawn to the cottage in the far distance, beyond the cart, in the mist. I certainly don't recall it and I would love to know something about it. Could it be Apple Tree Farm?

The turning into Greenwood Road, where the houses were beginning to appear little by little, is easy to see on the left, with the bakers' shop, then called Parkers, on the corner. There is a sign advertising 'teas' next to the door. The elegant doorway across the corner of the building is a similar style to the doorway of the bank on page 24. Sadly it was done away with in the destructive 60s and the pillars were replaced with fake marble-effect ones. Best not mentioned, perhaps.

The saddest feature of this picture is just beyond the bakers' shop where the large, almost windowless cottage is evident. This is Westonia Cottage, variously misspelt in a selection of publications. Sometimes it becomes Westoria, sometimes Wisteria, but in fact it is Westonia. The block of flats that now occupies the entire corner site has been named after it. Why is it sad? Because it was the first building in the village to be bombed on 3rd September, 1940. Three members of the family who lived therein died that day: Mr. and Mrs. D. G. Jones and their little girl, Valerie. Melville, their ten year old son survived to tell the tale.

Luckily, on this sunny day, no one foresaw the first Worle War, let alone the second.

HIGH STREET. WORLE.

38

It seems worthwhile including this picture, if only because it shows the dwellings along the north side of the street so clearly.

Beyond the tall boundary wall of the Lion, a lane runs up to the blacksmith's forge. Then there are a group of picturesque cottages, including Prospect Cottage, painted white in the picture, but now a very strong pink hue. Perhaps the most interesting house is 'Fairfield', built in late Georgian times as a single home and occupied by a series of families, including the May family who ran the Brewery and Malthouse featured on page 4. Sometime between 1871 and 1881 the Sawkins family moved in and stayed there until at least 1901, according to the censuses. The 20th century brought many changes, with the house being divided into two after the Martin sisters sold up in the 1950s, and most of the garden around the house as well as land belonging to Apple Tree Farm, was taken up in the building of Martin's Grove.

The lion is still sleeping, or looking on, above the pub door, but the trelliswork on the porch has gone. I must mention that the telegraph pole nearest to the camera is still there – the very one – it bends gently to the north to this very day.

'Silvercraig' has appeared on the corner of Coronation Road, and probably was lived in by the Matthews family when this was taken.

...And finally, 1953 and Manor House Farm in the snow.

To the west, we can see the trees and the buttercup field at the bottom of Spring Hill. Work has been carried out at the very bottom of the hill to improve access to the 'new' senior school. I'm afraid that insufficient note was taken of the spring that gave the hill its name, or of the resultant stream. The pipe never did an adequate job of re-directing the water, and the road often flooded thereafter.

There was no traffic and all was quiet on this snowy day. There is snow in the branches of the cherry tree on the right, in the Rows Gardens. The original Rows cottages have been demolished and a cul-de-sac of council owned houses have been built to house the people.

The gas lamps are still in place, but not for much longer. We are in the new Elizabethan Age, and matters must move on, but we have a host of memories. Thank goodness.